MW00580606

September 11
2001
words and pictures
by Veronica Lawlor

2010

for Laura
with love

vero press

was

in the subway when the second tower of the World Trade Center was hit. It seemed unreal that a terrorist attack was taking place in New York City. When I got out of the Union Square subway station, everyone was in a panic. A woman ran up to me and told me that the Pentagon had been hit as well.

I ran over to Fifth Avenue and saw people pointing down the street. Then I heard their screams. I looked downtown and witnessed the collapse of the first tower. A giant fell in mere seconds, spewing ash, steel and smoke. It was awesome and terrifying. People stared or walked around in complete shock. Our city was falling.

Visual chaos mixed with an eerie silence...

The second tower collapsed about a half hour later. I was drawing it when it happened. A woman near me screamed. We were all crying. It was too much for any of us to realize at that moment how many people had just died.

We were all simply thinking of our beloved Trade Center. Then the reality
began to dawn on us. We had just witnessed the death of thousands of
people in the space of two minutes. A mournful silence filled the streets.

Washington Square Park, usually so full of
energy, was filled with wandering people.
No one knew quite what to do as we stared at
the massive cloud of smoke that was once our
majestic World Trade Center. A few people in
the park began discussing the causes of the attack,
which strangely made me feel better.

Mostly we just stood there, watching the smoke...

...or comforting
each other.

We walked around
slowly, as
if in a trance.

We thought of our loved ones, and waited in long lines at telephone booths to call home and say, "I'm fine."

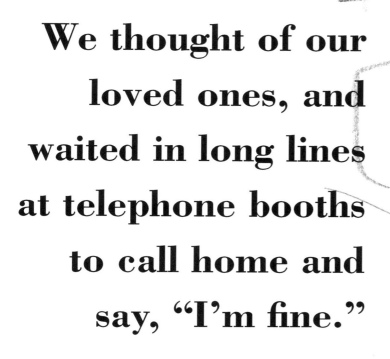

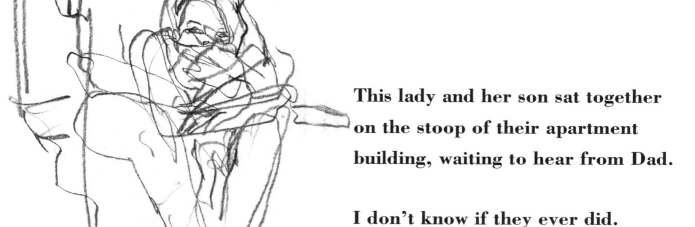

This lady and her son sat together on the stoop of their apartment building, waiting to hear from Dad.

I don't know if they ever did.

Soon we began to wake from our trance. People began moving faster, trying to get home. Nobody could use their cell phones to call families and say, "I'm alright," as all of the satellites had operated from the top of

the Twin Towers. The police started sectioning off parts of the streets downtown so the emergency vehicles, battered and covered with dust, could take what few survivors there were to area hospitals. There weren't many survivors to take.

And then

the workers from the Trade Center and the area around it began to appear along Broadway. Covered in soot, they staggered uptown, not really comprehending what they had seen and escaped. Suddenly we heard a woman crying hysterically. We all stopped and watched as a man, her husband, emerged from the cloud of smoke covered in ash, like someone raised from the dead. The couple embraced while the crowd cheered and cried with relief. At least one family avoided heartache that day. For too many other families, it was the beginning of the nightmare.

September 13, 2001

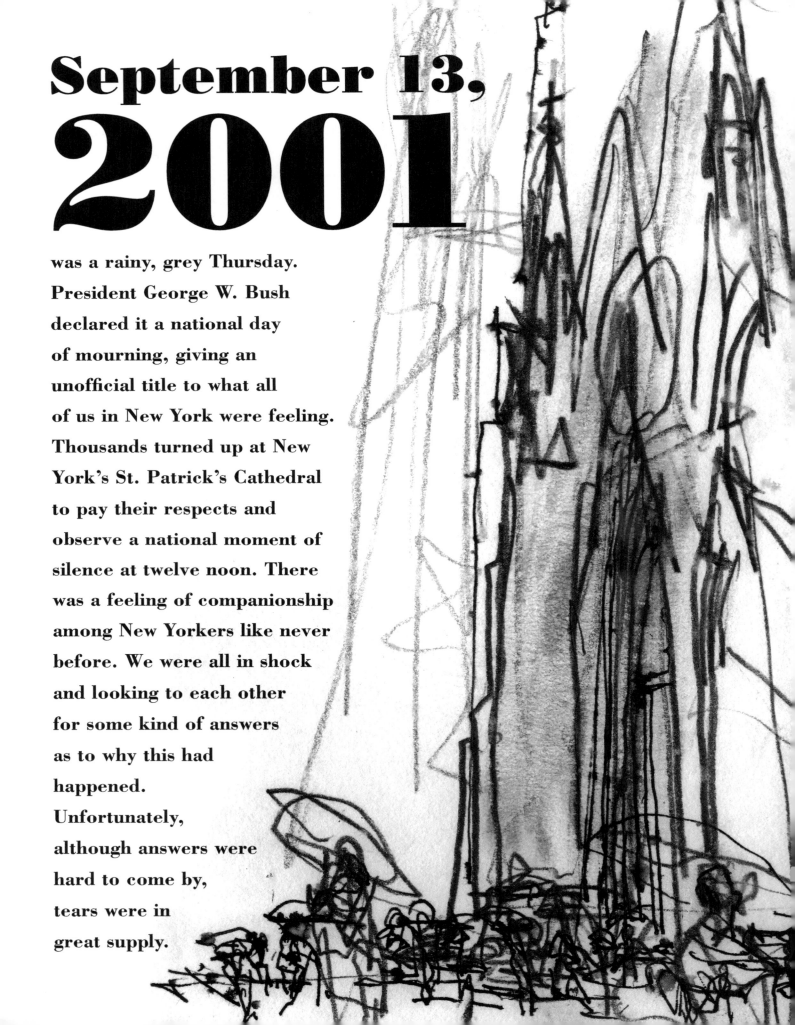

was a rainy, grey Thursday.
President George W. Bush
declared it a national day
of mourning, giving an
unofficial title to what all
of us in New York were feeling.
Thousands turned up at New
York's St. Patrick's Cathedral
to pay their respects and
observe a national moment of
silence at twelve noon. There
was a feeling of companionship
among New Yorkers like never
before. We were all in shock
and looking to each other
for some kind of answers
as to why this had
happened.
Unfortunately,
although answers were
hard to come by,
tears were in
great supply.

We went down to the site of what used to be our
World Trade Center. We stood, transfixed, and cried.
We couldn't believe our eyes.

Our city had been attacked, and all we could do was
stand there, looking at the devastation.

Workers
being
lowered
into the
wreckage

The workers toiled 24 hours a day. Members of the fire, police and transit department searched for their fallen comrades. Tons and tons of debris were carted out, and the bodies of the victims were recovered...slowly.

The city was closed off below 14th Street for days, while rescue workers sifted through the debris at the trade center site, hoping and praying to find survivors. Union Square Park became the site of the city's largest memorial, attracting crowds of people who came to pray, light candles, and write their thoughts on the long scrolls of white butcher paper that lined the pathways. Holy people of many religions offered public prayer services and the vigil for the missing continued every night, all night. Mixed in with the thoughts and prayers of the city were the missing persons posters, created by the families of the victims in hopes that someone, somewhere, would be found. It was a large funeral with the hope of a resurrection.

Poetry and
prayers
in Union Square

All the evidence

was pointing to Osama Bin Laden as the mastermind of the attacks. Muslims around the country came out in support of the United States and to denounce the Muslim extremists. One week after the attacks there was a press conference in Union Square. People of the Muslim, Jewish and Christian faiths alike spoke with concern, imploring government officials to lay the blame at the feet of the Taliban regime, not the innocent citizens of Afghanistan.

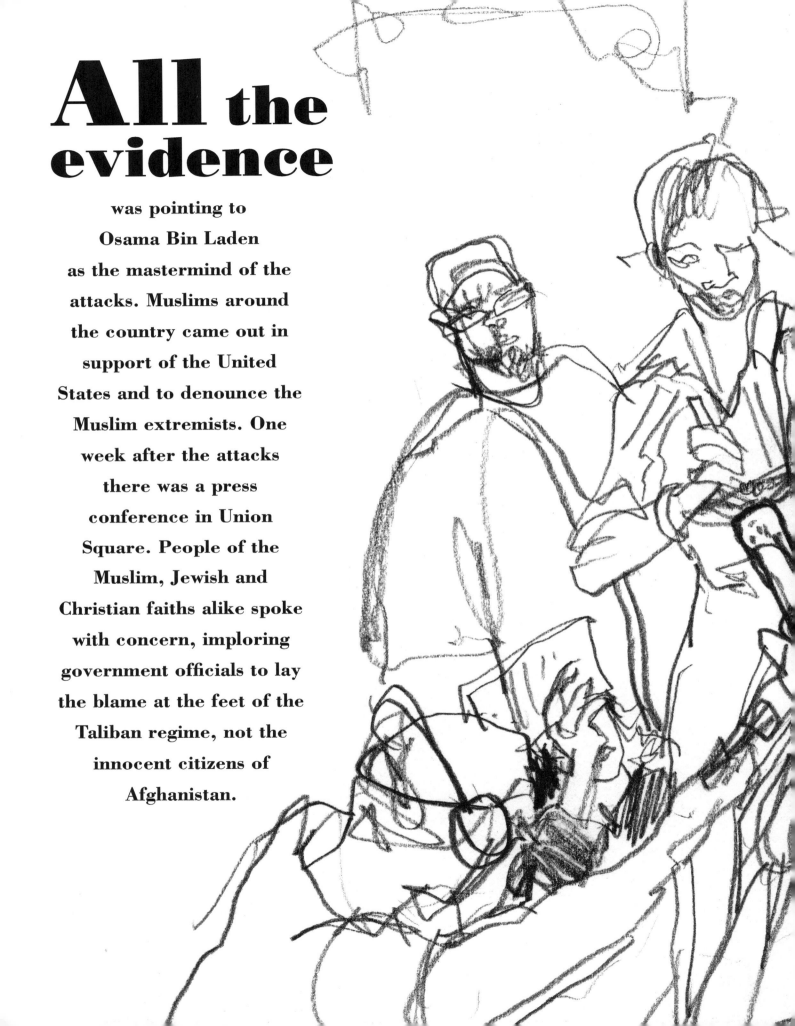

Across New York City

memorials sprung up for
the many firefighters, police and
transit workers who had given their
lives trying to save the people
trapped in the towers.
For the workers
who had survived there
were only questions and regrets.
Why did they die? Why didn't I?

It was hard to live with.
We could see the grief etched
in their faces and we had no
words of comfort to offer them.

We simply tried to be there
for them with our hearts, and show
them our gratitude for the service
they give to all of us in New York City
every day of the year.

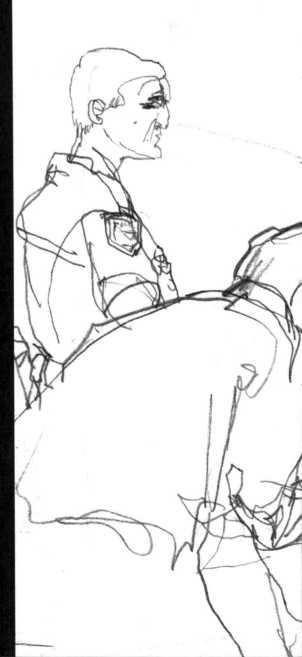

Help Arrives

From all across America volunteers and supplies came into New York City. The Javits Center in Manhattan was the unloading spot for thousands of blankets, gifts of food, clothing; anything that people displaced from their apartments and workers toiling at the site could need. The temperature at 'ground zero' was so hot that the rubber on the workers boots was melting every few hours. A woman in the Midwest made thousands of booties for the dogs walking among the wreckage, trained to sniff out signs of life. It was a wonderful feeling for New Yorkers to know that the rest of the country cared. Mayor Giuliani said he thought it was the first time New York City had ever really felt like a part of the United States. I agreed.

Some of the volunteers I met:

Terry, the Cantor Fitzgerald lady

The doctor from Indiana

The state trooper

The fire, police and transit workers were at the site 24 hours a day for weeks and weeks after the attack. They worked amid the ash and stench of the wreckage of our World Trade Center. Every day trucks loaded with the twisted steel of the Twin Towers drove out of the site.

rinsing off the trucks leaving the site

The workers did not want to stop looking for survivors, but eventually, hope grew faint. It became a point of honor for the workers at ground zero that they would at least recover the bodies of the fallen.

In public spaces around New York City the prayers continued.

Conspiracy theorists began to appear as well.

We prayed, we argued about politics, we wrote our feelings
out on large pieces of paper. But none of these things
could stop us from having to face the reality
that so many people who
went to work that
day would not
be coming home.

union square religiony

michael a christian lectures
on the similaries of all religion

Soon the funerals and the sound of bagpipes were common in the city.

Writing poetry, Times Square

St. Cecilia's Church, Brooklyn, New York

The funeral of Carl Bedigian.

Part Armenian, part Italian.

Married to my friend Michele.

A fireman of Engine 214,

Carl was one of over 300 firefighters who

perished on September 11th, 2001.

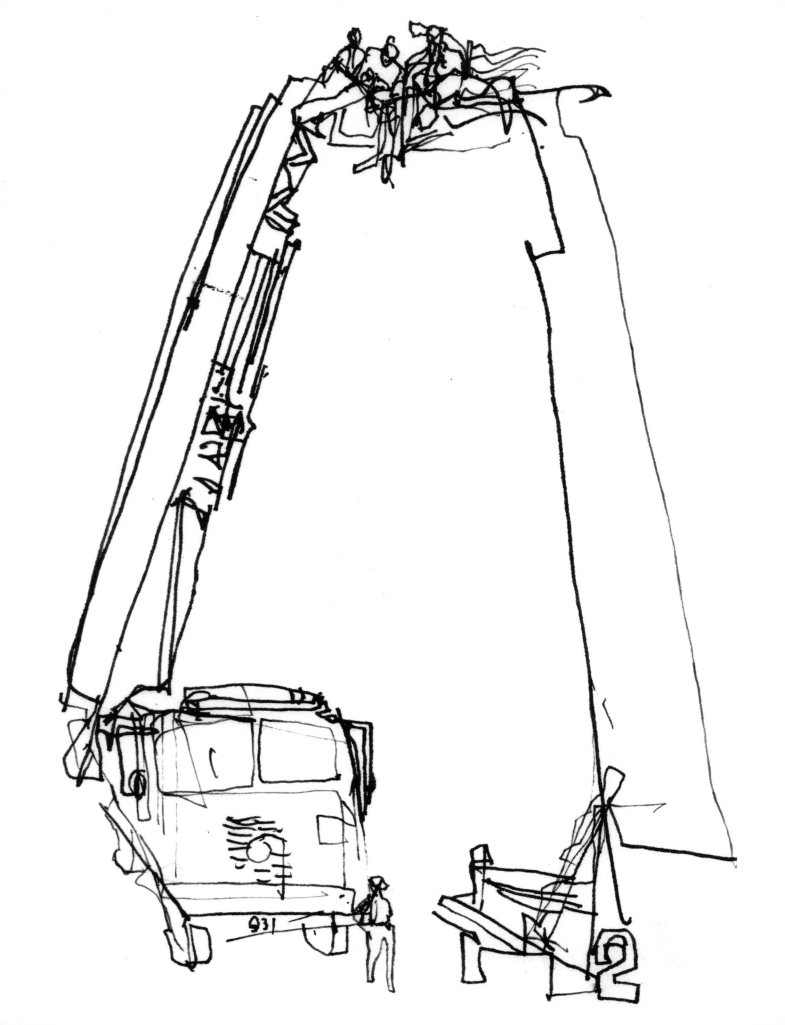

Carl never came home the day the Twin Towers

were attacked. He was found in the rubble of

Tower 2 several weeks later.

The other firemen arrive early on the

Monday morning of his funeral with the

ladder truck to hang a huge

American flag over the street.

Michele doesn't know what to do with his clothes.

I don't know what to tell her.

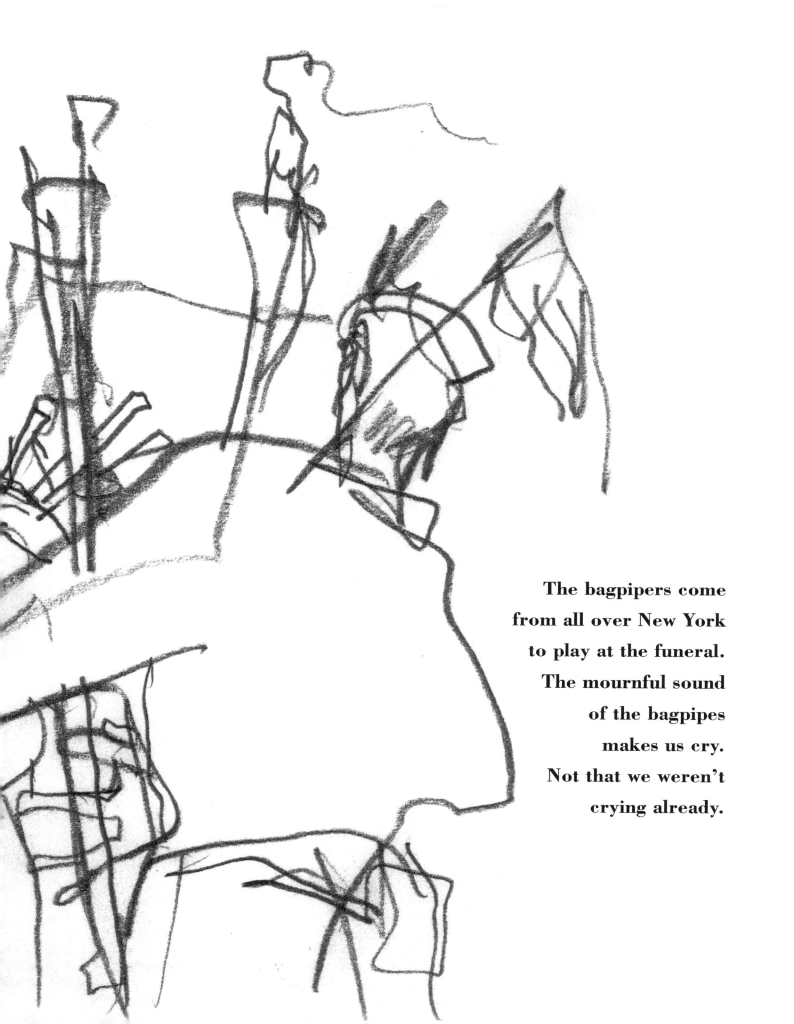

The bagpipers come
from all over New York
to play at the funeral.
The mournful sound
of the bagpipes
makes us cry.
Not that we weren't
crying already.

The service was so sad.
Michele called Carl "her angel."
They gave her his helmet,
and a flag.

She didn't look like Michele.

Carl Bedigian, Engine 214,

was laid to rest

on a cold, windy day in November.

Hundreds of firemen saluted in

silence as Carl's casket was

brought from the church and

placed on the fire truck for the

long, slow drive to the cemetery.

The truck stopped traffic on the

Brooklyn-Queens Expressway

as the rest of us followed behind.

Carl would have loved

to see the procession.

We wished he could have.

We can never forget.

New York, Washington, DC,
Shanksville, Pennsylvania and
the rest of America will always
remember Carl Bedigian
and the many other innocent
men and women who died on
September 11, 2001.
This book is for all of them.

*Author's note: since drawing these pictures in September 2001, I have
often been asked how I could possibly make drawings while these sad
and tragic events were happening. I can only say that, as a person who
communicates through art, how could I not draw what I was witnessing?
My country, my city, my family and friends were all under attack,
and it became increasingly important for me to document the events not only
of September 11th, but also of the days and weeks that followed.*

*This slim book does not claim to be a historically researched document
of the terrorist attacks of September 11th, 2001. It is merely one person's
account of a world-altering event. It is my hope that by publishing my words
and pictures, I can in some small way contribute to our understanding of what
happened in New York City, Washington, DC and Shanksville, Pennsylvania
on that beautiful September day, in ways both personal and public.*

Thanks to Michele Bedigian for sharing her story.
Thanks to Dominick Santise and Margaret Hurst for their assistance with this book,
and Neil Weisenfeld for his encouragement.

A portion of the proceeds from this publication will be donated to the New York Firefighters
Burn Center Foundation, in memory of Carl Bedigian. The New York Firefighters Burn Center is
dedicated to the advancement of burn care, research, prevention, education, and the proper
treatment of burns. For more information, please visit www.nyffburncenter.com.

For more information about Veronica Lawlor,
please visit www.studio1482.com/veronica or www.veronicalawlor.com.
To order this book, or for more information, please visit
www.sept11wordsandpictures.com.

LaVergne, TN USA
24 January 2010
170720LV00005B